This Summer Journal
Belongs to:

_____

The Year is:

_____

Summer adventures start here!

Summer Bucket List

Oh, the places I'd love to visit!

1. _____
2. _____
3. _____
4. _____
5. _____
6. _____
7. _____

Oh, the people I'd love to see!

1. _____
2. _____
3. _____
4. _____
5. _____
6. _____
7. _____

Oh, the things I'd love to do!

1. _____
2. _____
3. _____
4. _____
5. _____
6. _____
7. _____

*Location*_____*Date*_____

What I did today:

I really enjoyed:

One lesson from this day

_____

_____

One thing that made me smile

_____

_____

One special memory from this day

_____

_____

_____

Location_____Date_____

What I did today:

I really enjoyed:

One lesson from this day

One thing that made me smile

One special memory from this day

Location_____Date_____

What I did today:	I really enjoyed:

One lesson from this day

_____

_____

_____

One thing that made me smile

_____

_____

_____

One special memory from this day

_____

_____

_____

Location_____Date_____

What I did today: I really enjoyed:

One lesson from this day

_____

_____

One thing that made me smile

_____

_____

One special memory from this day

_____

_____

_____

Location_____Date_____

What I did today:

I really enjoyed:

One lesson from this day

_____

_____

One thing that made me smile

_____

_____

One special memory from this day

_____

_____

*Location*_____*Date*_____

What I did today:	I really enjoyed:

One lesson from this day

_____

_____

One thing that made me smile

_____

_____

One special memory from this day

_____

_____

Location_____Date_____

What I did today:	I really enjoyed:

One lesson from this day

_____

_____

_____

One thing that made me smile

_____

_____

_____

One special memory from this day

_____

_____

_____

Location_____Date_____

What I did today:

I really enjoyed:

One lesson from this day

_____

_____

One thing that made me smile

_____

_____

One special memory from this day

_____

_____

*Location*_____*Date*_____

What I did today:	I really enjoyed:

One lesson from this day

_____

_____

One thing that made me smile

_____

_____

One special memory from this day

_____

_____

Location_____Date_____

What I did today:

I really enjoyed:

One lesson from this day

_____

_____

_____

One thing that made me smile

_____

_____

_____

One special memory from this day

_____

_____

_____

Location_____Date_____

What I did today:

I really enjoyed:

One lesson from this day

_____

_____

_____

One thing that made me smile

_____

_____

_____

One special memory from this day

_____

_____

_____

*Location*_____*Date*_____

What I did today: I really enjoyed:

One lesson from this day

_____

_____

One thing that made me smile

_____

_____

One special memory from this day

_____

_____

_____

Location_____Date_____

What I did today:

I really enjoyed:

One lesson from this day

_____

_____

_____

One thing that made me smile

_____

_____

One special memory from this day

_____

_____

Location_____Date_____

What I did today:

I really enjoyed:

One lesson from this day

_____

_____

_____

One thing that made me smile

_____

_____

_____

One special memory from this day

_____

_____

_____

Location_____Date_____

What I did today:

I really enjoyed:

One lesson from this day

One thing that made me smile

One special memory from this day

Location_____Date_____

What I did today:	I really enjoyed:

One lesson from this day

_____

_____

One thing that made me smile

_____

_____

One special memory from this day

_____

_____

_____

*Location*_____*Date*_____

What I did today:

I really enjoyed:

One lesson from this day

_____

_____

_____

One thing that made me smile

_____

_____

_____

One special memory from this day

_____

_____

_____

Location_____Date_____

What I did today:

I really enjoyed:

One lesson from this day

_____
_____
_____

One thing that made me smile

_____
_____

One special memory from this day

_____
_____
_____

Location_____Date_____

What I did today:

I really enjoyed:

One lesson from this day

_____

_____

_____

One thing that made me smile

_____

_____

_____

One special memory from this day

_____

_____

_____

Location_____Date_____

What I did today:

I really enjoyed:

One lesson from this day

_____

_____

One thing that made me smile

_____

_____

One special memory from this day

_____

_____

_____

*Location*_____*Date*_____

What I did today:

I really enjoyed:

One lesson from this day

_____

_____

_____

One thing that made me smile

_____

_____

One special memory from this day

_____

_____

_____

Location_____Date_____

What I did today:

I really enjoyed:

One lesson from this day

_____

_____

One thing that made me smile

_____

_____

One special memory from this day

_____

_____

*Location*_____*Date*_____

What I did today:	I really enjoyed:

One lesson from this day

_____

_____

_____

One thing that made me smile

_____

_____

_____

One special memory from this day

_____

_____

_____

Location_____Date_____

What I did today:

I really enjoyed:

One lesson from this day

One thing that made me smile

One special memory from this day

Location_____Date_____

What I did today:

I really enjoyed:

One lesson from this day

One thing that made me smile

One special memory from this day

Location_____Date_____

What I did today:

I really enjoyed:

One lesson from this day

_____

_____

One thing that made me smile

_____

_____

One special memory from this day

_____

_____

_____

Location_____Date_____

What I did today:

I really enjoyed:

One lesson from this day

_____

_____

One thing that made me smile

_____

_____

One special memory from this day

_____

_____

*Location*_____*Date*_____

What I did today:	I really enjoyed:

One lesson from this day

_____

_____

One thing that made me smile

_____

_____

One special memory from this day

_____

_____

Location_____Date_____

What I did today:	I really enjoyed:

One lesson from this day

_____

_____

One thing that made me smile

_____

_____

One special memory from this day

_____

_____

*Location*_____*Date*_____

What I did today:

I really enjoyed:

One lesson from this day

_____

_____

One thing that made me smile

_____

_____

One special memory from this day

_____

_____

_____

Location_____Date_____

What I did today:	I really enjoyed:

One lesson from this day

_____

_____

One thing that made me smile

_____

_____

One special memory from this day

_____

_____

_____

*Location*_____*Date*_____

What I did today:

I really enjoyed:

One lesson from this day

_____

_____

One thing that made me smile

_____

_____

One special memory from this day

_____

_____

_____

Location_____Date_____

What I did today:

I really enjoyed:

One lesson from this day

_____

_____

_____

One thing that made me smile

_____

_____

_____

One special memory from this day

_____

_____

_____

Location_____Date_____

What I did today:

I really enjoyed:

One lesson from this day

One thing that made me smile

One special memory from this day

*Location*_____*Date*_____

What I did today:	I really enjoyed:

One lesson from this day

_____

_____

One thing that made me smile

_____

_____

One special memory from this day

_____

_____

Location_____Date_____

What I did today: I really enjoyed:

One lesson from this day

_____

_____

One thing that made me smile

_____

_____

One special memory from this day

_____

_____

_____

*Location*_____*Date*_____

What I did today:	I really enjoyed:

One lesson from this day

_____

_____

One thing that made me smile

_____

_____

One special memory from this day

_____

_____

Location_____Date_____

What I did today:	I really enjoyed:

One lesson from this day

_____

_____

One thing that made me smile

_____

_____

One special memory from this day

_____

_____

_____

Location_____Date_____

What I did today:

I really enjoyed:

One lesson from this day

_____

_____

One thing that made me smile

_____

_____

One special memory from this day

_____

_____

_____

Location_____Date_____

What I did today:

I really enjoyed:

One lesson from this day

_____

_____

One thing that made me smile

_____

_____

One special memory from this day

_____

_____

_____

Location_____Date_____

What I did today:	I really enjoyed:

One lesson from this day

_____

_____

_____

One thing that made me smile

_____

_____

_____

One special memory from this day

_____

_____

_____

Location_____Date_____

What I did today: | I really enjoyed:

One lesson from this day

_____

_____

One thing that made me smile

_____

_____

One special memory from this day

_____

_____

_____

Location_____Date_____

What I did today:	I really enjoyed:

One lesson from this day

_____

_____

One thing that made me smile

_____

_____

One special memory from this day

_____

_____

Location_____Date_____

What I did today: I really enjoyed:

One lesson from this day

_____

_____

One thing that made me smile

_____

_____

One special memory from this day

_____

_____

Location_____Date_____

What I did today:

I really enjoyed:

One lesson from this day

_____

_____

_____

One thing that made me smile

_____

_____

_____

One special memory from this day

_____

_____

Location_____Date_____

What I did today:

I really enjoyed:

One lesson from this day

One thing that made me smile

One special memory from this day

*Location*_____*Date*_____

What I did today:	I really enjoyed:

One lesson from this day

_____

_____

_____

One thing that made me smile

_____

_____

_____

One special memory from this day

_____

_____

_____

Location_____Date_____

What I did today:

I really enjoyed:

One lesson from this day

_____

_____

_____

One thing that made me smile

_____

_____

One special memory from this day

_____

_____

Location_____Date_____

What I did today:

I really enjoyed:

One lesson from this day

_____

_____

One thing that made me smile

_____

_____

One special memory from this day

_____

_____

_____

*Location*_____*Date*_____

What I did today:	I really enjoyed:

One lesson from this day

_____

_____

One thing that made me smile

_____

_____

One special memory from this day

_____

_____

*Location*_____*Date*_____

What I did today:	I really enjoyed:

One lesson from this day

_____

_____

One thing that made me smile

_____

_____

One special memory from this day

_____

_____

_____

Location_____Date_____

What I did today:

I really enjoyed:

One lesson from this day

_____

_____

One thing that made me smile

_____

_____

One special memory from this day

_____

_____

*Location*_____*Date*_____

What I did today:	I really enjoyed:

One lesson from this day

_____

_____

One thing that made me smile

_____

_____

One special memory from this day

_____

_____

_____

Location_____Date_____

What I did today:

I really enjoyed:

One lesson from this day

_____

_____

One thing that made me smile

_____

_____

One special memory from this day

_____

_____

*Location*_____*Date*_____

What I did today: | I really enjoyed:

One lesson from this day

_____

_____

One thing that made me smile

_____

_____

One special memory from this day

_____

_____

Location_____Date_____

What I did today:

I really enjoyed:

One lesson from this day

_____

_____

One thing that made me smile

_____

_____

One special memory from this day

_____

_____

_____

Location_____Date_____

What I did today:

I really enjoyed:

One lesson from this day

_____

_____

One thing that made me smile

_____

_____

One special memory from this day

_____

_____

Location_____Date_____

What I did today:

I really enjoyed:

One lesson from this day

_____

_____

One thing that made me smile

_____

_____

One special memory from this day

_____

_____

_____

Location_____Date_____

What I did today:

I really enjoyed:

One lesson from this day

_____

_____

One thing that made me smile

_____

_____

One special memory from this day

_____

_____

Location_____Date_____

What I did today:

I really enjoyed:

One lesson from this day

_____

_____

One thing that made me smile

_____

_____

One special memory from this day

_____

_____

Location_____Date_____

What I did today:	I really enjoyed:

One lesson from this day

_____

_____

One thing that made me smile

_____

_____

One special memory from this day

_____

_____

_____

*Location*_____*Date*_____

What I did today:

I really enjoyed:

One lesson from this day

_____

_____

_____

One thing that made me smile

_____

_____

_____

One special memory from this day

_____

_____

_____

Location_____Date_____

What I did today:	I really enjoyed:

One lesson from this day

_____

_____

_____

One thing that made me smile

_____

_____

_____

One special memory from this day

_____

_____

_____

Location_____Date_____

What I did today:

I really enjoyed:

One lesson from this day

_____

_____

One thing that made me smile

_____

_____

One special memory from this day

_____

_____

Location_____Date_____

What I did today:	I really enjoyed:

One lesson from this day

_____

_____

One thing that made me smile

_____

_____

One special memory from this day

_____

_____

_____

Location_____Date_____

What I did today:	I really enjoyed:

One lesson from this day

_____

_____

One thing that made me smile

_____

_____

One special memory from this day

_____

_____

_____

Location_____Date_____

What I did today:

I really enjoyed:

One lesson from this day

_____

_____

_____

One thing that made me smile

_____

_____

_____

One special memory from this day

_____

_____

_____

Location_____Date_____

What I did today:

I really enjoyed:

One lesson from this day

_____

_____

One thing that made me smile

_____

_____

One special memory from this day

_____

_____

Location_____Date_____

What I did today:

I really enjoyed:

One lesson from this day

_____

_____

_____

One thing that made me smile

_____

_____

One special memory from this day

_____

_____

_____

Location_____Date_____

What I did today: I really enjoyed:

One lesson from this day

_____

_____

One thing that made me smile

_____

_____

One special memory from this day

_____

_____

Location_____Date_____

What I did today:

I really enjoyed:

One lesson from this day

_____

_____

One thing that made me smile

_____

_____

One special memory from this day

_____

_____

_____

Location_____Date_____

What I did today: I really enjoyed:

One lesson from this day

_____

_____

_____

One thing that made me smile

_____

_____

_____

One special memory from this day

_____

_____

_____

*Location*_____*Date*_____

What I did today:	I really enjoyed:

One lesson from this day

_____

_____

One thing that made me smile

_____

_____

One special memory from this day

_____

_____

*Location*_____*Date*_____

What I did today:

I really enjoyed:

One lesson from this day

_____

_____

One thing that made me smile

_____

_____

One special memory from this day

_____

_____

Location_____Date_____

What I did today:

I really enjoyed:

One lesson from this day

_____
_____
_____

One thing that made me smile

_____
_____
_____

One special memory from this day

_____
_____
_____

Location_____Date_____

What I did today:

I really enjoyed:

One lesson from this day

_____

_____

_____

One thing that made me smile

_____

_____

_____

One special memory from this day

_____

_____

_____

Location_____Date_____

What I did today:

I really enjoyed:

One lesson from this day

_____
_____

One thing that made me smile

_____
_____

One special memory from this day

_____
_____
_____

Location_____Date_____

What I did today: I really enjoyed:

One lesson from this day

_____

_____

One thing that made me smile

_____

_____

One special memory from this day

_____

_____

_____

Location_____Date_____

What I did today:

I really enjoyed:

One lesson from this day

_____

_____

One thing that made me smile

_____

_____

One special memory from this day

_____

_____

_____

Location_____Date_____

What I did today:

I really enjoyed:

One lesson from this day

_____

_____

One thing that made me smile

_____

_____

One special memory from this day

_____

_____

_____

*Location*_____*Date*_____

What I did today:	I really enjoyed:

One lesson from this day

_____

_____

One thing that made me smile

_____

_____

One special memory from this day

_____

_____

_____

Location_____Date_____

What I did today:

I really enjoyed:

One lesson from this day

_____

_____

_____

One thing that made me smile

_____

_____

One special memory from this day

_____

_____

_____

Location_____Date_____

What I did today:

I really enjoyed:

One lesson from this day

_____

_____

_____

One thing that made me smile

_____

_____

One special memory from this day

_____

_____

_____

Location_____Date_____

What I did today:

I really enjoyed:

One lesson from this day

_____

_____

One thing that made me smile

_____

_____

One special memory from this day

_____

_____

*Location*_____*Date*_____

What I did today:	I really enjoyed:

One lesson from this day

_____

_____

_____

One thing that made me smile

_____

_____

_____

One special memory from this day

_____

_____

_____

Location_____Date_____

What I did today: I really enjoyed:

One lesson from this day

_____

_____

One thing that made me smile

_____

_____

One special memory from this day

_____

_____

*Location*_____*Date*_____

What I did today:

I really enjoyed:

One lesson from this day

_____

_____

_____

One thing that made me smile

_____

_____

One special memory from this day

_____

_____

_____

*Location*_____*Date*_____

What I did today:

I really enjoyed:

One lesson from this day

_____

_____

One thing that made me smile

_____

_____

One special memory from this day

_____

_____

Location_____Date_____

What I did today:

I really enjoyed:

One lesson from this day

_____

_____

_____

One thing that made me smile

_____

_____

One special memory from this day

_____

_____

_____

Made in the USA
Middletown, DE
25 June 2022

67774829R00051